The Story of
the Supremes

V&A Publishing

Contents

Performing 'Stop! In the Name of Love' on the
Supremes/Temptations NBC TV special,
TCB (Taking Care of Business), 1968.

Dreams Do Come True

Foreword by Mary Wilson

Rock and roll was something new and wild. It touched people, bringing countries together. In the latter part of the 50s the original pioneers, people like Little Richard, Chuck Berry and Jerry Lee Lewis, were all the rage. By the time 1960 rolled around female groups, such as the Chantels and the Shirelles, were very popular. We were four young ladies – Florence Ballard, Betty McGlown, Diane Ross and me, Mary Wilson – daring to dream at a time in America when ours seemed an 'impossible dream'. In mid-1958 we became the Primettes.

From the beginning we loved glamour. As the Primettes, we wore sweaters and pleated skirts. We could not afford much else, plus the look was inspired by one of our favourite groups of the day, Frankie Lymon & the Teenagers. We started making our own little dresses. We had all taken home economics in elementary school, so we would buy Brunswick and Butterwick patterns from the local Woolworths store in downtown Detroit. We were hoping that our dreams would come true.

Motown Records' Berry Gordy didn't sign us at first. I guess he didn't want a group of sixteen-year-old girls running around Hitsville. However, we persevered. One day in 1961 some producers stuck their heads out of Studio A, frantically looking for back-ups and hand-clappers. We screamed out in unison, 'We'll do it!' and the rest is history.

While Berry Gordy and his Hitsville created the 'Motown Sound', in the UK the Rolling Stones, the Dave Clark Five, Cliff Richard and the Animals, to name but a few, were also inspired. All of us baby-boomers the world over were hearing the sound of rock and roll. America embraced the Beatles and Great Britain embraced us, the Supremes, in 1964.

By then we were no longer four girls, but three. Betty had left in 1960 to get married and her replacement, Barbara Martin, followed the next year. When we signed our recording contract with Motown in 1961, we became a trio. It was Florence Ballard who chose the name the Supremes. Our first album, *Meet the Supremes*, shows the three of us in our cute little suits and white gloves, with white pearls also bought from Woolworths.

Once the hit records of Holland-Dozier-Holland started coming, so did the clothes! When we received our royalty cheques we could go shopping at the likes of Saks Fifth Avenue. Then, with each No.1 hit, we would have designers send us sketches of the most beautiful gowns. That's how the Mary Wilson gown collection first began and it has been in my possession all these years, proof that dreams really do come true.

Mary Wilson

Through the Window of Window of Lost Time: The Supremes, Motown Records and the American 60s

The Primettes' first single, 'Tears of Sorrow', was released on the Lupine label in 1960, with 'Pretty Baby' on the B side.

'Honey, we is terrific.'

Flo Ballard, Supreme

The success of the Supremes and Motown Records with black and white
audiences alike reflects the tumultuous history of 60s America. The appearance
of the group in American living rooms during this period of quicksilver change
subliminally assisted in the creation of a more progressive social environment.
Although they were not overtly political themselves, every time Diana Ross,
Florence Ballard and Mary Wilson – three African-American women from
housing projects on the wrong side of Detroit – appeared in their fantastic new
outfits or their fresh-from-the-showroom Cadillacs, it was as potent as any
statement delivered by a political activist. The group acted like a chiffon
battering ram, defeating the enemy by singing his song, enticing the
mainstream with well-honed charisma and charm.

As flagship artists on Berry Gordy Jr's Detroit-based Motown Records label,
the Supremes stand alone. They became the most successful girl group of all
time and, in their leader Ross, introduced one of the true musical superstars of
the twentieth century. The original blend of Ballard, Wilson and Ross is one of
the most recognizable in popular music. They scored 12 US No.1 hits,
numerous Top 40 entries and record sales of over 20 million. Today, many still
regard them as the greatest female vocal group in pop history. 'The
Supremes were brittle, crystalline, hard as cut glass and as polished as
any of the sequins on Diana's skin-tight dresses. They took high
class about as high as it would go,' writer Mick Farren argued
in 1977. And, of course, the higher the class, the more lowly
the beginnings . . .

Diana Ross was born Diane Earle on 26 March 1944. After
moving to the Brewster-Douglass housing projects in Detroit
as a teenager, she began to sing with her friends Mary Wilson
(b. 6 March 1944), Betty McGlown (b. 1943) and Florence
Ballard (b. 30 June 1943, d. 22 February 1976) in their
group, the Primettes, female foils to the Primes, two of whom
were soon to become the Temptations. Through Ross's former
neighbour Smokey Robinson, the Primettes auditioned for local
entrepreneur Berry Gordy's label in 1960. Although he was
impressed, he told the four girls to work on their music and come back

LUPINE

Record Co., 3490 W. Boston Blvd.
Detroit 6, Mich.

LUP 1
Time: 2:15
Lupine Music
BMI

A Ham-Rich
Productions

TEARS OF SORROW
(Rich Morrison)
THE PRIMETTES
LR120

7

when they had graduated from high school. After replacing McGlown with Barbara Martin and recording a single, 'Tears of Sorrow', for the Lupine label, the Primettes still eyed Motown as their ideal home.

They were right, because even at this stage Gordy was clearly on to something in Detroit. So much has been written about the label that it is often difficult to get beyond the statistics, the scale of his achievement, and take things back to the music. There is no doubt that the later success of the Supremes sealed the success of Motown. The label had been founded in Detroit in 1959 by ex-boxer Gordy, who'd made a name for himself by writing for local singing legend Jackie Wilson. He'd wanted an imprint on which to put out all the music that excited him. After a slow start and experiments in jazz, blues and doo-wop, the label began to find a signature style.

The Primettes were finally accepted by Motown in late 1960, recording the Gordy, Brian Holland and Freddie Gorman-penned 'I Want a Guy', which was released on 9 March 1961. However, their name was considered inappropriate by Gordy. Even though the girls came up with sheets of possible alternatives, it wasn't until contracts were being drawn up that Ballard finally made her decision. She plumped for the Supremes, because everything else they had considered seemed to end in an '-ette'. Wilson and Ross initially felt the name a bit too masculine for the group.

'I Want a Guy' and their seven subsequent releases did very little in the US pop or R&B charts. After their second release, the Ballard-led 'Buttered Popcorn', Barbara Martin departed in summer 1961, leaving the group as a trio. Their 1962 single, 'Your Heart Belongs to Me', full of writer Smokey Robinson's wistful allusions to a lover overseas ('serving your country on some faraway sand'), saw them just dint the US Top 100, but it wasn't enough to stop the group being known as the 'no-hit Supremes' at Motown's offices.

By 1963, Motown was beginning to get into its stride. Every Tuesday, International Talent Management Incorporated would meet and discuss each group's development, touring schedules and personal appearances. Every Friday, the Product Evaluation Committee would listen to the new records that had been made during the week and pass judgement on what should happen to them next. The Supremes were to become the star pupils at the recently opened Motown finishing school, learning how to behave and how to exploit their photogenic looks. The Motown Artist Development Division, or 'charm school', was run by Maxine Powell, who had had her own finishing and modelling school in Detroit for some years. It taught the artists manners, etiquette and stage presence. The mission was simple, as Powell told author Gerard Early: artists should 'be able to dine and converse with kings and queens'. And, although they were trailing badly in comparison with other

The Primettes, with Barbara Martin front left, 1961.

Motown artists such as the Marvelettes and Mary Wells, Gordy sincerely believed that the Supremes were heading for top-flight clubs and lounges across the US.

the success of the Supremes sealed the success of Motown

Gordy, who had singled out Ross's breathy, vulnerable style for lead vocals, instructed his in-house song-writing team of brothers Brian and Eddie Holland and Lamont Dozier to work with the trio. Immediately, they began to craft songs that suited the group's range. 'Florence was the lead singer,' Lamont Dozier told writer Brian Chin in 2001, 'but Diana had the tools. Vocally, her appearance, her whole attitude . . . she had a presence about her.' By late 1963 and their first Top 40 hit, 'When the Lovelight Starts Shining through His Eyes', Ross had assumed all A-side lead duties for the group. And then, the following year, the floodgates finally opened. 'Where Did Our Love Go', initially disliked because of its repetitive simplicity, was offered to the group after being turned down by the Marvelettes. Recorded in April and released in June 1964, it topped the US charts as well as reaching No.3 in Britain. It has been heard almost too many times to be fully appreciated, but it undoubtedly remains one of the sweetest moments in pop.

With its permanent spring-like blast, upbeat and optimistic, 'Baby Love' was the track that underlined the Supremes' superstardom. The Funk Brothers, talented musicians of the Detroit studios' 'snakepit', provided some of their

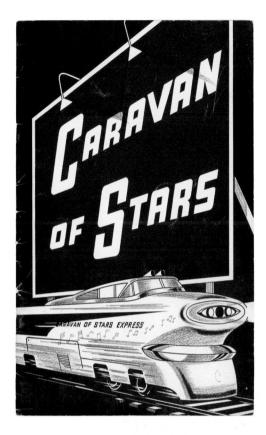

Souvenir programmes for the
Caravan of Stars tour, 1964, and
'A Night with the Supremes', 1966.

Early publicity photograph of the Supremes taken
by Tony Spina of the Detroit Free Press.

Inner record sleeve showing the range of Motown fan products on offer, late '60s.

deftest commercial backings for the girls. 'Come See about Me' became their third US No.1 in six months. It topped the charts for a week before being deposed by the Beatles' 'I Feel Fine', and then returned to the summit in early 1965. *The Virgin Encyclopedia of Popular Music* noted, 'with their girl-next-door looks and endearingly unsophisticated demeanour, the Supremes became role models for young black Americans'.

Cover of sheet music for 'Stop! In the Name of Love', 1965.

In themselves the girls carried no great social or philosophical weight – for example, they hurried out of their first and only ever meeting with the Beatles in New York in 1965: 'We felt we had interrupted something,' Mary Wilson later said, while George Harrison recounted, 'We expected soulful, hip girls. We couldn't believe that three black girls from Detroit could be so square.' But it was their unfinished nature – downtown girls making it in beautiful clothes – that helped propel them to the heart of the mainstream. They even had a bread named after them: a picture from this period shows the three girls chomping on a pure-white slice. However, Gordy was also acutely aware of the adult market the group was gaining and had them release albums such as *We Remember Sam Cooke* and had their live show recorded from the heart of the US establishment, New York's legendary Copacabana Club.

'Stop! In the Name of Love', released in February 1965, continued the Supremes' remarkable run of hit releases. This was serious pop, sequinned, pristine, porcelain almost. Melvin Franklin from the Temptations suggested the famous hand gesture at the start of the record for performances, giving them their iconic pose. The Supremes were seen to be reaping their just rewards for putting in tremendously hard work. Everything they did in this imperial phase was watchfully supervised by Maxine Powell, Gordy and choreographer Cholly Atkins. Gil Askey became the group's arranger and Maurice King their musical director. Atkins took their uncultured clumsiness and taught them the beautiful value of economy, so that by 1966 their slightest on-stage gesture seemed to carry a remarkable amount of meaning.

Their success was worldwide. From the moment the Supremes landed in London – where they appeared on *Ready Steady Go!* – in October 1964, they were treated like royalty, and Diana Ross remains to this day the fullest embodiment of the word 'diva'. In the UK, Motown was seen as something of a delicacy. Mary Wilson said in her autobiography, *Dreamgirl*, 'In the beginning, they referred to us as "negresses", a term we had never heard. At first, we were offended... As we began to understand the English, we saw there was no offence intended. We were exotic darlings, sexy and cute, and all the more interesting because we were black and hailed from what the foreign press liked to portray as a rat-infested ghetto.' They were part of the fabled Tamla-Motown tour in March 1965, where all the key players on Motown's roster came over and were greeted by serious-minded, bespectacled enthusiasts who knew facts about the label that the performers themselves had long forgotten.

By this time, after the phenomenal success of its charges the Miracles, the Temptations and the Supremes, Motown had become the largest independently owned record company in America and the country's most financially successful African-American business. Gordy had a remarkable understanding of art and commercialism, and his belief in the Supremes was simply amazing. In July 1966, he issued a memo to the Motown staff: 'We will release nothing less than Top 10 products on any artists. And because the Supremes' worldwide acceptance is greater than the other artists', on them we will only release No.1 records.' Four straight No.1s were to follow: 'You Can't Hurry Love', 'You Keep Me Hanging On', 'Love Is Here and Now You're Gone' and 'The Happening'. The group went to Europe and the Far East. By the end of the year, they were megastars, appearing on countless TV shows, and were voted by *Playboy* readers the No.1 pop group, ahead of the Beatles. However, Ross was already being groomed for stardom away from the group and in 1966 Diane Ross announced to the world that she was now to be known as 'Diana'.

The Supremes' story took place against the backdrop of one of the most turbulent decades in US history. As the 60s commenced, there was still widespread racial segregation and discrimination in the South; war was raging in Asia and America was entering a period of introspection. In 1960, John Kennedy had been elected to the White House. As Gordy's first wife, Raynoma, was later to say, 'We watched him and his beautiful wife on television and felt only more hope – for the country, for our little company and for ourselves.' JFK had taken a new approach to civil rights, with his implicit backing of the Rev. Martin Luther King Jr and, as a result, garnered 75 per cent of the African-American vote in the presidential election. Now there were pressing matters to deal with.

Although the bus boycotts had led to segregated buses being declared unconstitutional, in the South unofficial laws kept segregation in place. Freedom rides – buses with integrated passengers – started off from Washington and headed south. The first bus was set on fire, the second attacked by the Ku Klux Klan. Kennedy's brother Robert replaced the buses. In Montgomery all hell broke loose, with rioting, deaths and subsequent imprisonments.

European record sleeve for 'Where Did Our Love Go', the Supremes' first No.1 in both the US pop and R&B charts, 1964.

The photograph used on the cover of the group's second album, *Where Did Our Love Go*, was also the front cover of this programme for the Supremes' 1965 tour.

At a time when freedom rides were fraught with danger, Gordy decided to take his Motown artists on a tour bus through different states. The Miracles and the Temptations later recalled suffering insults and ignominies as they hit the South, and according to Diana Ross, 'In practically every city, we couldn't find a restaurant that would let us come in the front door, and we were determined not to have to use the back door.' The gigs would be segregated by ropes, blacks on one side and whites on the other.

Mass marches followed and JFK put the first Civil Rights bill to Congress in February 1963; it failed. On 28 August 1963, Martin Luther King addressed a crowd of 250,000 in front of the Lincoln Memorial, Washington, DC, with his 'I Have a Dream' speech. After Kennedy's assassination in November 1963, his successor, Lyndon Johnson, passed the Civil Rights Act the following year, outlawing discrimination, enlarging federal powers to protect voting rights and, in theory, speeding school desegregation in the process.

The radical African-American leader Malcolm X was gunned down in February 1965, just as Motown Records really began to consolidate their success. 'I knew that an age of terrible violence and suffering had just begun,' Marvin Gaye was to tell author David Ritz. The Voting Rights Act became law on 6 August 1965, removing all legal barriers to enfranchising African-Americans. A handful of days later, the Watts Riots erupted in Los Angeles. In 1966, Stokely Carmichael called for 'black power' and the Black Panther party was formed. The late 60s saw increasing divisions over the best way to achieve black economic and social advancement. Although the right noises were being made, the pace of change was slow for the man in the street and the after-effects of racism were to be felt for a considerable time longer.

By 1967, things were changing for the Supremes. Their tenth US No.1, 'The Happening', was released in May of that year, the final record to be credited to the Supremes. Gordy had made little secret of the fact that he saw Diana Ross as the group's leader; now there was the suggestion that, at some point in the not too distant future, she would strike out on her own. 'We were in England when the first rumours came out about Diane leaving the group,' Mary Wilson was later to say. 'I think it was the *Daily Mail* that asked. We were sitting there going, Ahhhh. Florence and I were very angry about Diane being pulled out. We were never consulted, and suddenly Diane was moving forward, the Supremes pushed back.' Flo Ballard – 'Blondie' – the original lead vocalist who'd been such a driving force in the early days of the group, had begun to miss shows and argue with Ross. She would have to be dealt with as a matter of haste. Ballard made her final appearance with the group in Las Vegas in July 1967 (Cindy Birdsong from Patti LaBelle and the Bluebells was brought in to replace her).

Classic poster for the Supremes' concert at the Lincoln Center, New York. V&A: E.323–1973

'Reflections', the final record on which Ballard sang and the first credited to Diana Ross and the Supremes, showcased the entire Motown writing, production and singing team at its very best. Set against the rioting in North America, the escalation of troop deployment in Vietnam, war in the Middle East and the emergence of China as a nuclear power, it was arguably Holland-Dozier-Holland's finest moment. In the new, free-love hippie society, this was the trio's response, a three-minute stab at rhapsody. 'With all the psychedelic stuff coming in,' Lamont Dozier said, 'we put the oscillator on the front of the song, and it just worked perfectly. It was our answer to the new medium of psychedelic music.'

The lyrics spoke of lost hope and became a soundtrack to the era:

Through the
hollow of
my tears I
see a dream
that's lost
From the hurt
That you
have caused

In you I put
All my faith
and trust
Right before
my eyes
My world
has turned
to dust

The Supremes released two studio albums with the Temptations,
the second, *Together*, featuring this stunning poster artwork.

This bittersweet love song was a comment from H-D-H through their purest mouthpieces to a troubled America. Martha Reeves and the Vandellas' 'Dancing in the Street' had been appropriated by rioters and the Temptations' 'Get Ready' was seen as a call to assimilation, but there was still no overtly political statement from the label. 'Reflections' reached No.2 in the US charts, kept off the No.1 spot by the Box Tops' 'The Letter'.

Between 22 and 27 July 1967, the riots in Detroit claimed the lives of 43 people and saw 7,000 arrested. Motown had received anonymous death threats when the Supremes and the Four Tops played a concert in New York sponsored by a white-owned beer company. The studio was spared but closed for the six-day period of rioting. By the end of the 60s, Berry Gordy had moved his operations out to the west coast of America.

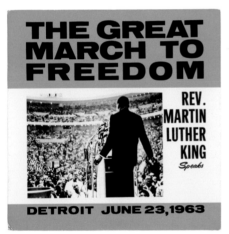

Cover of the first of four albums of Martin Luther King's speeches, released by Motown in 1963.

In April 1968, Martin Luther King was assassinated in Memphis. James Brown's actions after that night have been well documented: he played a televised concert in Boston and made direct pleas to quell civil disturbance. Less dramatic but more wide-reaching were the words of Diana Ross, who was performing with the Supremes on Johnny Carson's *The Tonight Show* the night after King's murder. Ross spoke, alone, on a chat show for the first time. Her speech was delivered falteringly, but the message was clear: 'I'm very sad. And I'm angry too, but I don't think it's good to be angry. I really don't know what to say . . . all I can say is what's inside. I'm here and I respected and loved Dr Martin Luther King very much. And I know he lived and died for one reason – and I want all of us to be together. Not just the black man but the white man and everybody.' The Supremes also attended the funeral and burial of King, and, later that summer, they endorsed Hubert Humphrey, the centrist Democrat opponent to Richard Nixon.

Inspired by the street politics of the Black Panthers, music became edgy, freedom-tinged. Gordy's approach was simply to allow talent to flourish. This itself was his ultimate political statement. He was there at the march on Washington; he'd released speeches by Martin Luther King. Yet Motown, and the Supremes in particular, seemed increasingly incongruous. The politicization of 'Reflections', 'Love Child' or 'The Young Folks' was tempered with 'The Impossible Dream' with the Temptations. Although loaded with meaning post-King, it was still a sweet showbiz salvo. And then, songs like 'For Better or Worse', with suggestions of taking breakfast to her man's bed, wrote the dichotomy large. As Peter Doggett put it in his book *There's a Riot Going On*, with the Supremes, 'for every slice of down-home grit, there was an album of Broadway standards and Beatles covers to swallow'.

'The times were definitely changing,' wrote Mary Wilson in *Dreamgirl*, 'and being accomplished, world-famous black women, the Supremes were caught in cross-fire between standard show-business conventions and new, more radical ideas about performers as political spokespeople and leaders . . . though we'd never shunned political or social issues, we were starting to take a beating for being glamour girls in a "relevant" age. The press would accept some other pop stars' cries for revolution at face value, never bothering to note that these stars lived as lavishly as we did. But the Supremes were right out there and before long we'd be attacked in the press for not being black enough.' It was left to Motown writer and producer Norman Whitfield to make some of the label's most political music, before the male leads Marvin Gaye and Stevie Wonder finally stopped being part of the Hit Machine and began saying what they really felt in the early 70s.

Holland-Dozier-Holland left Motown acrimoniously over unpaid royalties, yet the Supremes' hits kept coming. When the group had a residency at London's glittering Talk of the Town in January and February 1968, they were again treated like royalty – a party was thrown in their honour by the Duke and Duchess of Bedford in Chelsea, with guests including Mick Jagger, Michael Caine, Lynne Redgrave, Vanessa Redgrave, Paul McCartney, Tom Jones and Marianne Faithfull. To promote their September 1968 release, 'Love Child', which was penned by a collection of Gordy's writers to keep them at the top of the charts, the group appeared barefoot in Afros on *The Ed Sullivan Show.* This was a reflection of the changing times. 'Love Child' knocked 'Hey Jude' off the No.1 spot in the US charts.

By the end of the 60s, some of the most progressive and also the most devastating developments in US history had taken place. The Civil Rights movement had made considerable advances. The country was still at war in Vietnam, and it had lost three influential leaders to assassins: John Kennedy, Martin Luther King and Robert Kennedy.

The Supremes had run out of impetus and by 1970 Mary Wilson was the sole original member of group. Two mammoth NBC spectaculars uniting the Temptations and the Supremes – the Primes and the Primettes – were aired, and as the second, *GIT (Getting It Together on Broadway)*, was shown in November 1969, the final Diana Ross and Supremes record, 'Someday We'll Be Together', raced to the US No.1 spot and became the final chart-topper of the American 60s.

After a huge farewell gig at the Frontier Hotel in Las Vegas on 14 January 1970, Jean Terrell replaced Ross as the group's lead vocalist. Ross had simply become too famous to be constrained by her old group. Her time with the Supremes ended in a blaze of flashbulbs and she went on to become one of the

they
bridged
white
conservatism
and
black
radicalism

world's best-known superstars. Meanwhile, the Supremes' line-up changed frequently, with Lynda Laurence, Scherrie Payne and Susaye Greene all becoming members. They enjoyed chart success, with an extremely respectable run of hits, but finally split up in 1977. It was all over. As with their closest rivals, the Beatles, the story of the Supremes was contained almost entirely in the 60s. There was a preamble in the 50s and a denouement in the 70s, but everything important happened in those ten years.

The Supremes' achievements are legendary. Even in today's pop- and 'celebrity'-saturated culture, few groups have had an exhibition at one of the world's most prestigious museums. This in addition to previous honours such as being the first African-Americans on the cover of any weekly TV magazine; opening the '8th Wonder of the World', the Houston Astrodome, with Judy Garland in 1965; and having Gemini 5 astronauts Charles 'Pete' Conrad and Gordon Cooper request to hear 'Where Did Our Love Go' from Gemini Control in August 1965. Black poet Gil Scott Heron was later to bemoan 'Whitey on the Moon', but at least there had been Supremes in space. They were the first African-American group to perform at the prestigious Copacabana Club in New York (29 June 1965); they were the first pop group to perform at the Lincoln Center's Philharmonic Hall (15 October 1965). The group was at the very heart of the musical establishment.

The Supremes had acted as a populist soundtrack to the 60s in America and in doing so they bridged white conservatism and black radicalism. Although there had been girl groups before, no one had performed quite so definitively, so triumphantly. From Destiny's Child to the Sugababes, their influence today is clear. As noted by Charles Shaar Murray in Q magazine back in 1987, their songs of 'devotion, dependence and disappointment' were playing when Martin Luther King marched on Washington, when man landed on the moon, when Detroit burned, and then, a few years later, they were gone.

If what we are left with now is ultimately a selection of very posh frocks, they still embody all of the glamour, the poise and the panache of this fabled, troubled era. These were the dresses that helped make history. These were the work clothes of being a Supreme.

Daryl Easlea

Cover of sheet music for 'Love is Like an Itching in My Heart',
written by Holland-Dozier-Holland and released in 1966.

The History of the Supremes

This range of record covers shows the Supremes at their sartorial best.

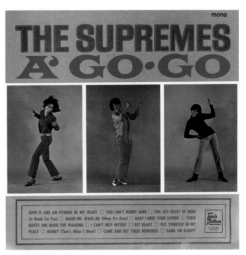

Diana

Previously unpublished, the following three solo photographs of the Supremes were taken by Harry
Goodwin at BBC Television Centre in London, while the group was preparing for *Top of the Pops*, *c*.1965.

Florence

'Just a few months before we were eating crummy road food in an old bus; now we were flying first-class, drinking champagne, and eating caviar.'

Mary Wilson

Front cover from the programme for 'An Evening with the Supremes', 1966.

JEDE WOCHE NEU:

Ein Tip für Autogrammjäger: Einfach die Autogramm-Marke auf di
Kuverts kleben und an folgende Adresse schicken (Frankieren und d
Antwortschein nicht vergessen!):

The Supremes, 2648 West Grand Boulevard, Detroit 8, Michigan, USA

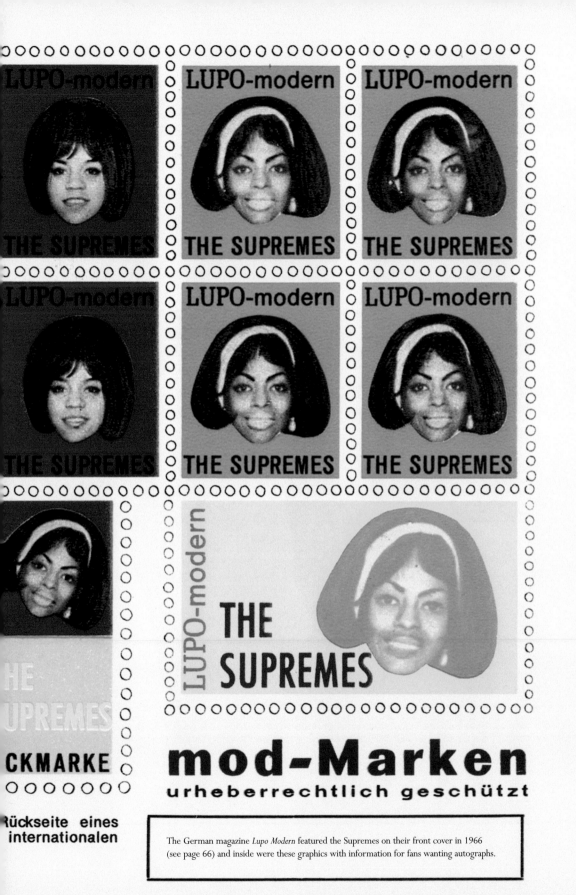

The German magazine *Lupo Modern* featured the Supremes on their front cover in 1966 (see page 66) and inside were these graphics with information for fans wanting autographs.

'The artists
were diamonds
in the rough,
and Motown
had the good
sense to
polish them.'
Maxine Powell

The Supremes meeting Queen Elizabeth, the Queen Mother, at the
Royal Variety Performance at the London Palladium, 1968.

"THE SUPREMES"
DIANA ROSS · FLORENCE BALLARD · MARY WILSON
(Biography)

In 1964, a nation of teenagers, disc jockeys, and just plain music lovers, all turned into "astronomers." For suddenly, three new stars, Diana Ross, Mary Wilson and Florence Ballard, clustered like diamonds into one shining group called The Supremes, caught fire. Their records began selling at a phenomenal rate, resulting in The Supremes being awarded nine gold records in a period of less than two and a half years, for "Where Did Our Love Go," "Baby Love," "Come See About Me," "Stop In The Name Of Love," "Back In My Arms Again," "I Hear A Symphony," "You Can't Hurry Love," "You Keep Me Hanging On" and "Love Is Here And Now You're Gone," all of which sold a million or more records and soared to the top of the pop record charts.

Diana

Mary

Florence

Back and inside front cover from the programme for 'An Evening with the Supremes', 1966.

43

The Supremes, 1968.

The photograph on the sheet music for 'Love Child' comes from the group's appearance on *The Ed Sullivan Show* on 29 September 1968. 'Love Child', the second single they released after the departure of songwriters Holland-Dozier-Holland, was their first No.1 without them.

Cover of sheet music for 'Someday We'll Be Together', the final Supremes record
featuring Diana Ross, 1969.

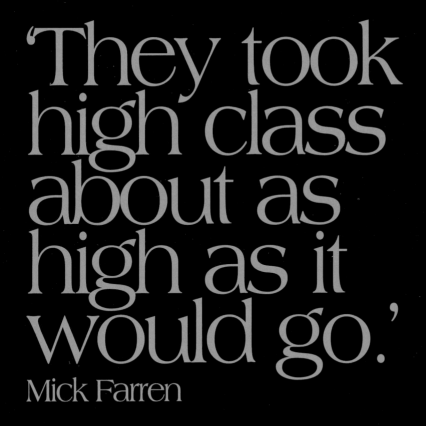

'They took high class about as high as it would go.'
Mick Farren

A classic Supremes pose by legendary New York photographer James J. Kriegsmann.

Previously unpublished photograph by Harry Goodwin from the Supremes'
appearance on *Top of the Pops*, c.1965

The Supremes in Japan, 1966.

Backstage photograph of the Supremes preparing for a concert
at the Venetian Room in the Fairmont Hotel, San Francisco.

The Supremes being photographed at the headquarters
of EMI Records in London's Manchester Square, 1964.

Best of Everything' Supremes

Diana Ross

Lot of Happiness Florence

Mary

A mass-produced 'signed' Supremes Fan Club photograph.

The Supremes in San Francisco.

Previously unpublished photograph showing the Supremes as they were about to be photographed
by Harry Goodwin, taken by Ron Howard, Harry's assistant on *Top of the Pops*, c.1965.

TAMLA-MOTOW

- **THE SUPREMES** • **SMOKEY R**
- **MARTHA AND THE VANDELLAS**

The Motown invasion was announced with a UK tour in 1965
after the Tamla-Motown London-based label had been established.

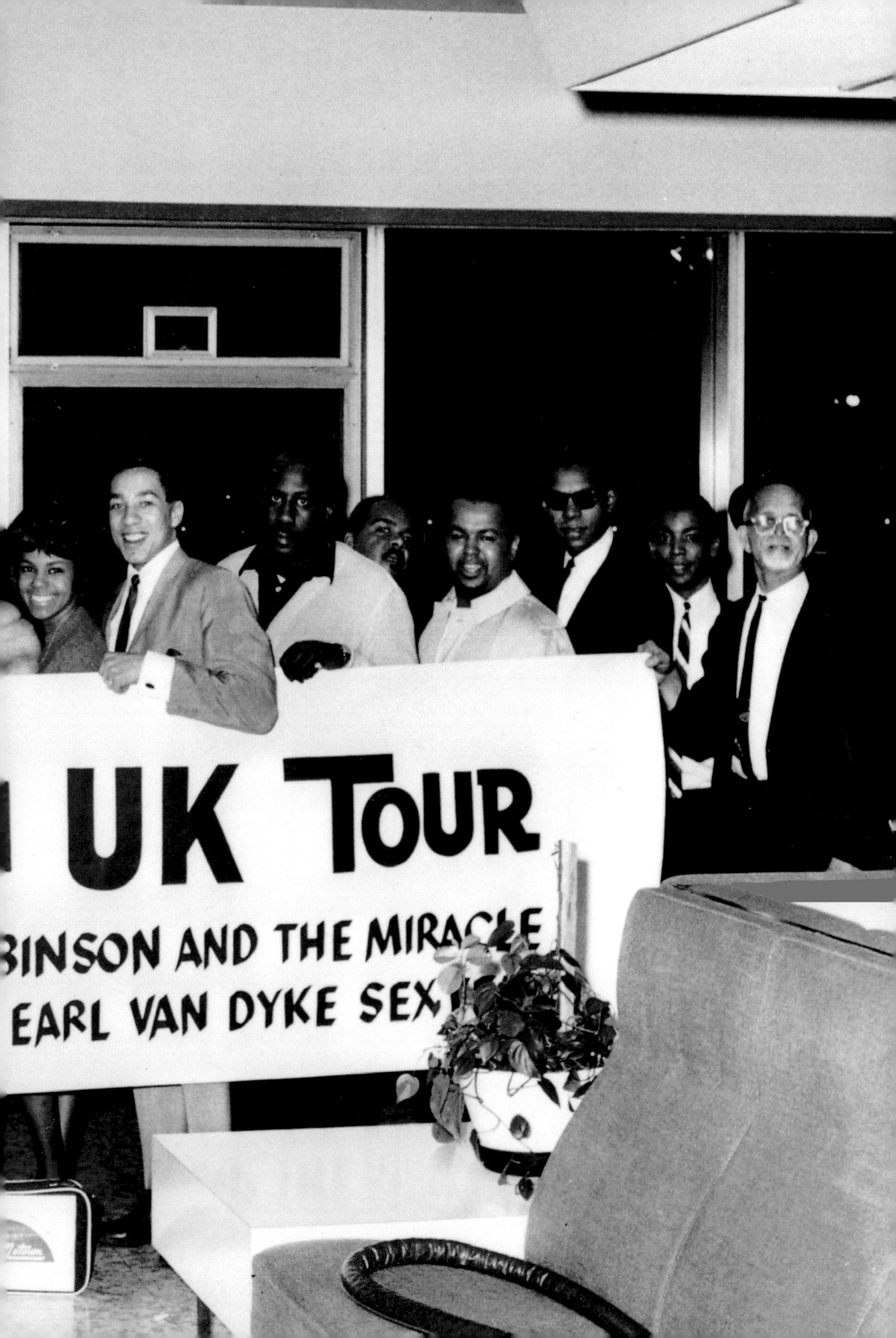
UK TOUR
BINSON AND THE MIRACLE
EARL VAN DYKE SEX

The Supremes at London's Heathrow Airport, 1965.

The Supremes on the front cover of *Lupo Modern*, 1966.

US advertisement for the album *The Supremes Sing Holland-Dozier-Holland*, 1967.

The Supremes on tour: in Paris in 1965 (left) and in London in 1964 (right).

The Supremes arrive at London's Heathrow Airport, 1965.

'With their girl-next-door looks and endearingly unsophisticated demeanour, the Supremes became role models for young black Americans.'

The Encyclopedia of Popular Music

'They...embody all of the glamour, the poise and the panache of this fabled, troubled era.'

Daryl Easlea

Berry Gordy and the Supremes preparing for a *Hullabaloo* TV special in the NBC studio at Midwood, Brooklyn, *c.*1965.

"I can honestly say that Diana Ross and The Supremes are not only magnificent performers .:. but they happen to be marvelous ladies."
SAMMY DAVIS, JR.

"...I loved the clear, pure sound and the joy that was an inherent part of their music, and I was immediately converted as a fan."
GENE KELLY

"Great as The Supremes are on records, they are even greater in person.'
CAROL CHANNING

"The femme trio . . . are stirring the kind of action at the B.O. generally associated with the Sammy Davises and Frank Sinatras."
HERM/VARIETY

"For the capacity audience the trio could do no wrong . . . brilliant production, great choreography."
CLAUDE HALL/BILLBOARD

"The three young ladies turned in a convincing demonstration of why they reign Supremes."
PETE JOHNSON/LOS ANGELES TIMES

"I have witnessed five (5) great theatrical experiences in my lifetime, and The Supremes' Coming Home was one of them."
DICK OSGOOD, WXYZ
VETERAN ENTERTAINMENT CRITIC

"You-all are my favorite group and I love you-all so much."
LYNDA B. JOHNSON
CENTURY PLAZA HOTEL
HOLLYWOOD, CALIFORNIA

"The Supremes are Michigan's most exportable product."
REP. JOHN CONYERS QUOTING
GOVERNOR ROMNEY OF MICHIGAN

OUTSTANDING SINGLES
"I Want A Guy" ■ "Buttered Popcorn" ■ "Breathtaking Guy" ■ "Lovelight In His Eyes" ■ "Where Did Our Love Go" ■ "Baby Love" ■ "Come See About Me" ■ "Stop In The Name Of Love" ■ "Back In My Arms Again" "Nothing But Heartaches" ■ "I Hear A Symphony" ■ "My World Is Empty Without You" ■ "Love Is Like An Itching In My Heart" ■ "You Can't Hurry Love" ■ "You Keep Me Hangin' On" ■ "Love Is Here And Now You're Gone" ■ "The Happening" ■ "Reflections" ■ "In And Out Of Love"

ALBUMS
"The Supremes Sing Country, Western & Pop" ■ "Meet The Supremes" ■ "Where Did Our Love Go" ■ "The Supremes Sing A Bit Of Liverpool" ■ "The Supremes — We Remember Sam Cooke" ■ "More Hits by The Supremes" ■ "Supremes At The Copa" ■ "Merry Christmas — The Supremes" ■ "I Hear A Symphony" ■ "Supremes A Go-Go" ■ "Supremes Sing Holland-Dozier-Holland" ■ "Supremes Sing Rodgers and Hart" ■ "Diana Ross and The Supremes Greatest Hits"

OUTSTANDING ENGAGEMENTS
Holiday Acres/Norfolk, Virginia ■ Olympia Music Hall/Paris, France ■ Cobo Hall/Detroit, Michigan ■ Steel Pier/Atlantic City, New Jersey ■ Cow Palace/San Francisco, California ■ Grand Gala Du Disque/ Amsterdam, Holland ■ Philharmonic Hall/ Lincoln Center, New York ■ McCormick Place/Chicago, Illinois ■ Kiel Auditorium/ St. Louis, Missouri

CLUBS
Clay House Inn/Bermuda ■ Twenty Grand Lounge/Detroit, Michigan ■ Copacabana/ New York ■ Safari Room/San Jose, California ■ Blinstrub's/Boston, Massachusetts ■ Latin Casino/Cherry Hill, New Jersey ■ Twin Coaches Club/Pittsburgh, Pa. ■ Eden Roc Hotel/Miami, Florida ■ Roostertail/Detroit, Michigan ■ Deauville Hotel/Miami, Florida ■ Flamingo Hotel/Las Vegas, Nevada ■ O'Keefe Centre/Toronto, Canada ■ Fairmont Hotel/San Francisco, California

TELEVISION APPEARANCES
London Palladium/London, England ■ Steve Allen ■ Ed Sullivan ■ Les Crane ■ Shindig ■ Hullabaloo ■ Hollywood Palace ■ Mike Douglas ■ Red Skelton ■ Dean Martin ■ Sammy Davis, Jr. ■ Shivaree ■ Tonight ■ Anatomy of Pop ■ What's My Line ■ Tarzan TV Series

MOTION PICTURES
"TAMI" Film ■ "Beach Ball" ■ Title Song — "Dr. Goldfoot and the Bikini Machine"

Inside spread from a Supremes concert programme, 1967.

Rehearsing 'Baby Love' at the *Top of the Pops* studio in
Manchester for the show broadcast on 15 October 1964.

The Supremes on *The Ed Sullivan Show*, 1968.

One of the many photographs of the Supremes taken in London in 1964; a similar image was used for the cover of the album *A Bit of Liverpool* released that year.

A James J. Kriegsmann photograph of the Supremes, 1968.

'And Flo, she doesn't know…' sings Diana Ross in this 1965 *Hullabaloo* TV
performance of 'Back in My Arms Again', the group's fifth consecutive No.1.

'These were the dresses that helped make history. These were the work clothes of being a Supreme.'

Daryl Easlea

Bibliography

Brewster, Bill, and Broughton, Frank, *Last Night a DJ Saved My Life: The History of the Disc Jockey* (London, 1999)

Bronson, Fred, *The Billboard Book of Number 1 Hits* (updated and expanded 5th edition, New York, 2003)

Doggett, Peter, *There's a Riot Going On: Revolutionaries, Rock Stars and the Rise and Fall of 60s Counter-Culture* (Edinburgh, 2007)

George, Nelson, *Where Did Our Love Go? The Rise and Fall of the Motown Sound* (London, 1986)

Guillory, Monique, and Green, Richard C. (eds), *Soul: Black Power, Politics and Pleasure* (New York, 1998)

Larkin, Colin (ed.), *The Virgin Encyclopedia of Popular Music* (concise 4th edition, London, 2002)

Marsh, Dave, *The Heart of Rock and Soul: The 1001 Greatest Singles Ever Made* (London, 1989)

Ritz, David, *Divided Soul: The Life of Marvin Gaye* (London, 1986)

Ross, Diana, *Secrets of a Sparrow: Memoirs* (London, 1993)

Taraborrelli, J. Randy, *Call Her Miss Ross: The Unauthorized Biography of Diana Ross* (London, 1989)

Taraborrelli, J. Randy, with Darryl Minger and Reginald Wilson, *Diana: The Life & Career of Diana Ross* (London, 1985)

Ward, Brian, *Just My Soul Responding – Rhythm and Blues, Black Consciousness and Race Relations* (London, 1998)

Werner, Craig, *A Change Is Gonna Come: Music, Race and the Soul of America* (Edinburgh, 2000)

Wilson, Mary, with Patricia Romanowski and Ahrgus Juilliard, *Dreamgirl: My Life As a Supreme* (London, 1987)

Acknowledgements

V&A Publishing would like to acknowledge the following: first, Mary Wilson, without whom the exhibition and accompanying book would never have happened; then, from the Victoria and Albert Museum, Geoff Barlow, Victoria Broackes, Clare Davis, Vanessa Eyles, Anjali Kothari, Zoe Louizos, Geoffrey Marsh, Laura Shaw, Clare Taylor and Damien Whitmore; from Storey London Design, Andy Bannister and Mike Storey; everybody who helped with sourcing images, including Sonia Buchholz, Harry Goodwin, Juliette Losardo (Getty Images), John O'Connor, Gilles Pétard and especially Eric Charge, for access to his incredible collection and his help with the captions; from the United States, Richard Duryea and Howard Kramer (Curatorial Director of the Rock and Roll Hall of Fame); from the Universal Music Group, Daryl Easlea, Lori Froeling, Jeff Koenig, Michael Reinert and Harry Weigner; and, finally, our wonderfully calm and collected editor, Lesley Levene.

Picture Acknowledgements (numbers refer to pages): Eric Charge Collection: 11, 52, 64–5; Getty, Hulton Archive: 1, 40, 54–5, 72–3, 86–7; Getty, Michael Ochs Archives: front cover, 2, 4, 9, 12–13, 44–5, 48, 57, 60–61, 62–3, 80–81, 84–5, 88, 89, 90–91, 96; Harry Goodwin, photographer's collection (www.harrygoodwin.com): 30, 33, 34, 50–51, 58–9; Gilles Pétard Collection: 6; Motown, courtesy of Motown Records Archive: 15, 22, 27, 46–7, 69, 70–71, 75, 76–7, 82–3, 94, back cover; Motown, Eric Charge Collection, courtesy of Motown Records Archive: 11, 17, 37, 42–3, 53, 56, 67, 68; Motown, private collection, courtesy of Motown Records Archive: 14, 16, 21, 23, 28–9; Mary Wilson and the Estate of Joe Eula, Theatre Collection V&A Museum (V&A Images): 18.

First published by V&A Publishing, 2008
V&A Publishing
Victoria and Albert Museum
South Kensington
London SW7 2RL

Distributed in North America by Harry N. Abrams, Inc., New York

782.42 EAS

ISBN 978 185177 5521
Library of Congress Control number 2008924015

EXCAT

10 9 8 7 6 5 4 3 2 1
2012 2011 2010 2009 2008

A catalogue record for this book is available from the British Library.

Design: Storey London Design Ltd - www.storeylondondesign.co.uk
Copy-editor: Lesley Levene

Printed in Italy by Graphicom, a FSC certified company.

V&A Publishing
Victoria and Albert Museum
South Kensington
London SW7 2RL
www.vam.ac.uk

Mixed Sources
Product group from well-managed
forests, and other controlled sources
www.fsc.org Cert no. CQ-COC-000015
© 1996 Forest Stewardship Council

The Supremes performing 'Come See about Me' on *The Ed Sullivan Show*, 1964.